YOUR NEIGHBOR THE
MOUSE

GREG ROZA

WINDMILL
BOOKS

New York

Published in 2012 by Windmill Books, An Imprint of Rosen Publishing
29 East 21st Street, New York, NY 10010

First Edition

Editor: Jennifer Way
Layout Design: Greg Tucker

Photo Credits: Cover, pp. 4, 5, 6, 7, 9, 10–11, 13, 14, 15 (top, bottom), 17 (top), 18, 19, 20 Shutterstock.com; p. 8 © Stephen Dalton/age fotostock; p. 12 David Maitland/Getty Images; p. 16 © www.iStockphoto.com/Elena Milevska; p. 17 (bottom) Robin Redfern/Getty Images; p. 21 iStockphoto/Thinkstock; p. 22 Jeffrey Coolidge/Getty Images.

Library of Congress Cataloging-in-Publication Data

Roza, Greg.
 Your neighbor the mouse / by Greg Roza. — 1st ed.
     p. cm. — (City critters)
 Includes index.
 ISBN 978-1-4488-4998-7 (library binding) — ISBN 978-1-4488-5125-6 (pbk.) —
 ISBN 978-1-4488-5126-3 (6-pack)
 1. Mice—Juvenile literature. I. Title.
 QL737.R6R74 2012
 599.35′3—dc22
                                    2010049644

Manufactured in the United States of America

For more great fiction and nonfiction, go to www.windmillbooks.com

CPSIA Compliance Information: Batch #BS2011WM: For Further Information contact Windmill Books, New York, New York at 1-866-478-0556

CONTENTS

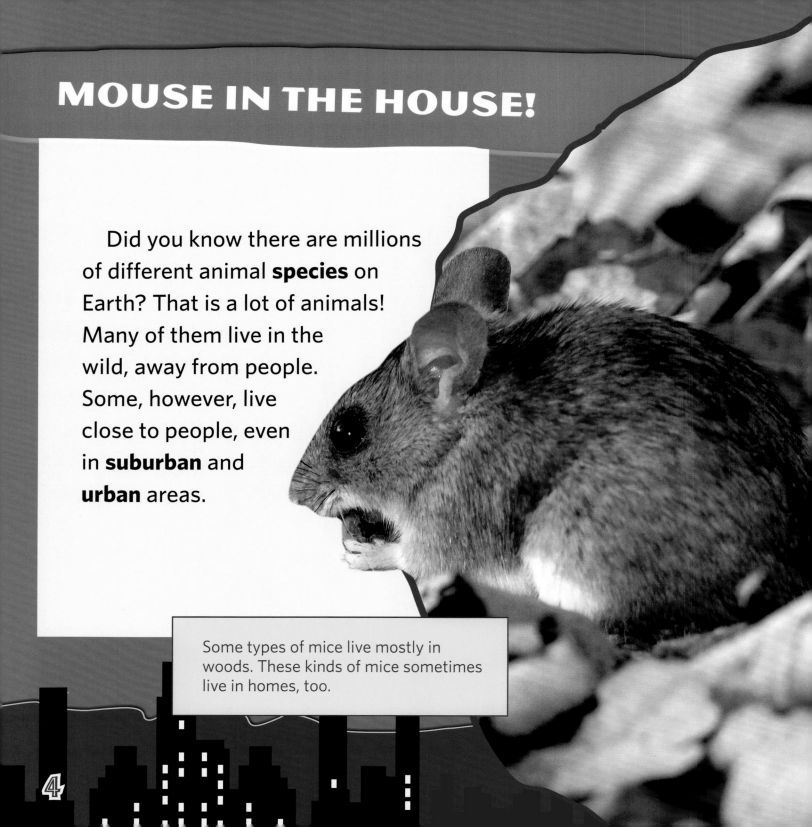

MOUSE IN THE HOUSE!

Did you know there are millions of different animal **species** on Earth? That is a lot of animals! Many of them live in the wild, away from people. Some, however, live close to people, even in **suburban** and **urban** areas.

Some types of mice live mostly in woods. These kinds of mice sometimes live in homes, too.

The house mouse is one of the most commonly found wild animals in towns and cities. As its name suggests, the house mouse often lives in houses with people. This might be good for the mouse, but it can be bad for people!

Mice may be found in parks, in homes, and anywhere people are.

MICE ARE RODENTS

The scientific name for a house mouse is *Mus musculus*. House mice are rodents, which is the largest group of **mammals** on Earth. Rodents have four large front teeth. They **gnaw** wood to keep their teeth sharp. House mice use their teeth to open nuts, dig tunnels, and **defend** themselves from enemies. House mice are active mainly at night.

Mice that do not live in people's homes may dig holes in the ground, in which they make their homes.

House mice are only about 2.5 to 4 inches (6–10 cm) long. Their tails are often longer than their bodies. House mice have light brown to black fur. They have white or gray fur on their bellies.

Mice will eat any food that is left out. These mice are feasting on a piece of bread.

WHAT'S ON THE MENU?

House mice are **omnivores**, which means they eat both plants and animals. In the wild, they eat seeds, roots, leaves, bugs, and sometimes dead animals. House mice are often found anywhere grain and hay are stored. This

House mice can fit through small holes they gnaw in walls.

makes them a big problem for farmers, feed stores, and markets.

Since many house mice live in homes, they often gnaw into boxes of food. They will get into open garbage cans, too. Along with people's food, house mice have been known to eat pet food, soap, glue, and other things in houses!

Mice are omnivores that will eat pretty much anything that people eat. This mouse is eating blackberries.

RAISING A FAMILY

In the wild, house mice can live for up to about two years. They are ready to **mate** by the time they are just five to seven weeks old. When looking for a mate, male house mice make a squeak so high-pitched that while people cannot hear it, female mice can.

House mice **reproduce** quickly. Males and females mate

Mice come in many different colors, such as white, black, and brown.

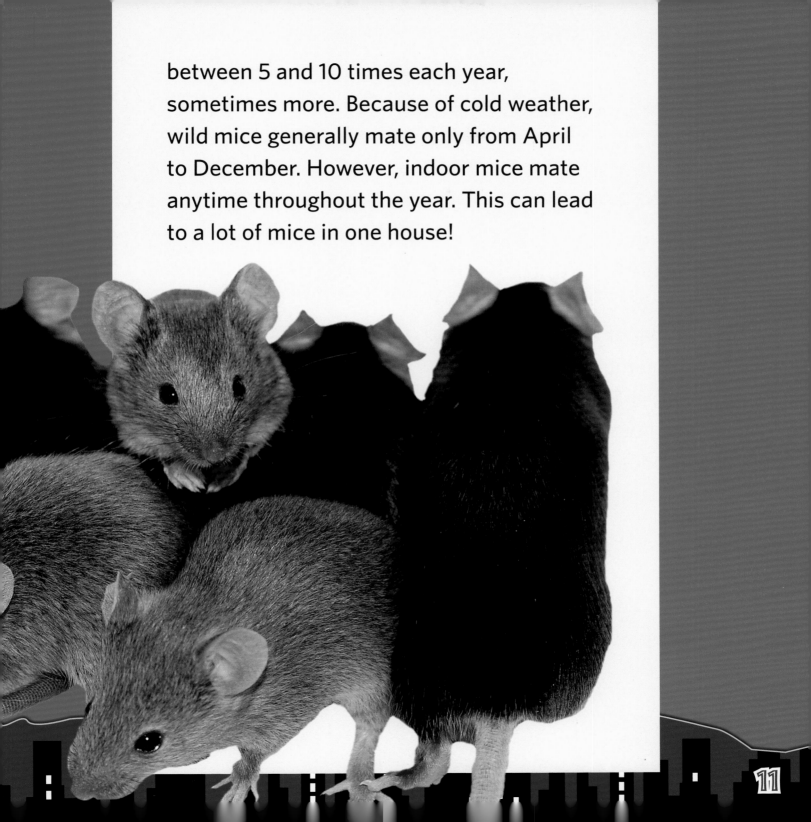

between 5 and 10 times each year, sometimes more. Because of cold weather, wild mice generally mate only from April to December. However, indoor mice mate anytime throughout the year. This can lead to a lot of mice in one house!

BABY MICE

After mating, female house mice make nests out of soft objects, generally bits of paper and cloth. Several females may share a nest if space is tight. Female house mice give birth about 19 to 21 days after mating.

Newborn mice pups are completely helpless. They cannot see or hear, and they have no fur.

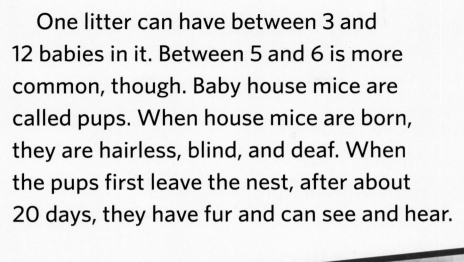

One litter can have between 3 and 12 babies in it. Between 5 and 6 is more common, though. Baby house mice are called pups. When house mice are born, they are hairless, blind, and deaf. When the pups first leave the nest, after about 20 days, they have fur and can see and hear.

As they begin to grow a bit, baby mice start to move around. These pups are moving around even though they are still blind and hairless.

IN THE WILD

House mice have followed people wherever they have settled. They came with people on ships and then moved into the homes they built. In this way, mice have spread to towns and cities everywhere. Thanks to people, house mice can live in areas where they would not otherwise be able to **survive**. These areas include deserts and **tundras**.

Mice will eat just about any food that they can get. This mouse is taking food from a bird feeder.

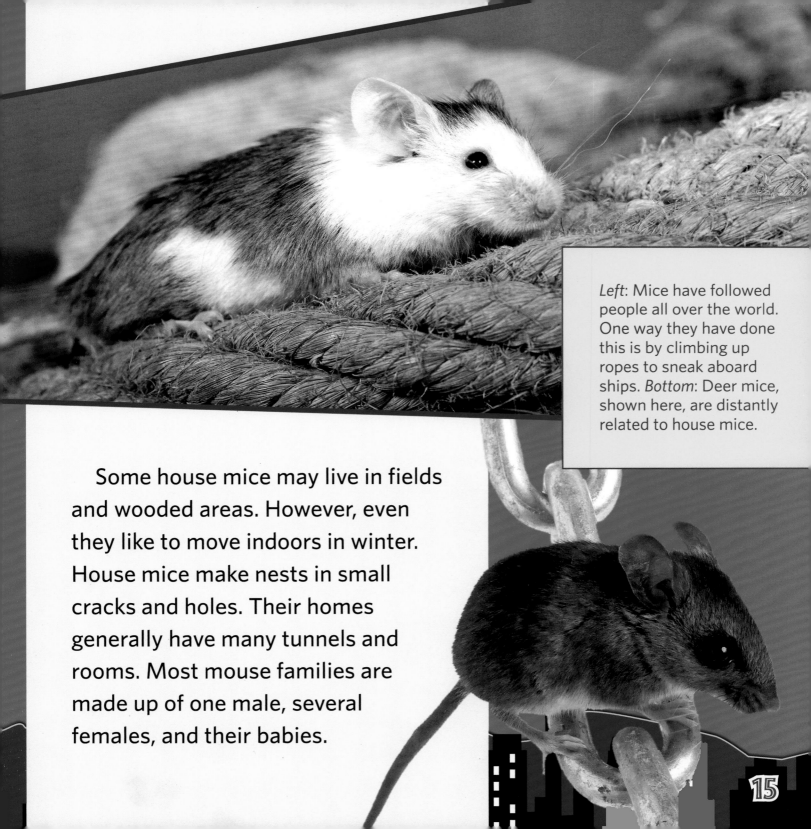

Left: Mice have followed people all over the world. One way they have done this is by climbing up ropes to sneak aboard ships. *Bottom*: Deer mice, shown here, are distantly related to house mice.

Some house mice may live in fields and wooded areas. However, even they like to move indoors in winter. House mice make nests in small cracks and holes. Their homes generally have many tunnels and rooms. Most mouse families are made up of one male, several females, and their babies.

MICE IN YOUR NEIGHBORHOOD

House mice are quick for their size. They can run up to 8 miles per hour (13 km/h)!

People have long kept pet cats to get rid of house mice.

House mice are not picky eaters. They can make a mess of your cupboards and garbage cans.

Even though they are very small, you might be able to hear house mice crawling behind your walls. The more there are, the louder they get!

Do the boxes of food in your cupboards have holes in them? If so, you likely have mice!

The best way to keep house mice out of your house is to cover all open holes and fill in cracks. When they have nowhere to build their nests, they will go somewhere else.

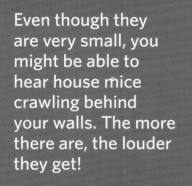

House mice love to gnaw wood. A home with house mice often has holes in its walls and floors.

MOUSE DANGER

In the wild, the house mouse has many **predators**, including foxes, weasels, lizards, snakes, and birds. A house mouse's greatest defense is its quickness and **agility**. House mice are also good swimmers, so they might be able to escape by swimming.

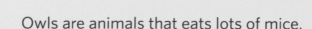

Owls are animals that eats lots of mice.

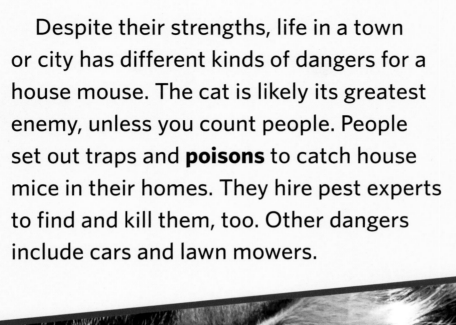

Despite their strengths, life in a town or city has different kinds of dangers for a house mouse. The cat is likely its greatest enemy, unless you count people. People set out traps and **poisons** to catch house mice in their homes. They hire pest experts to find and kill them, too. Other dangers include cars and lawn mowers.

Cats are well known for hunting and catching mice.

MICE AND PEOPLE

House mice generally do not go far from buildings. Food there is plentiful. Homes are warm in cold weather and dry in wet weather. Mice make nests by gnawing through wood, floor tiles, and even electrical wires. This can damage a home and make it unsafe.

Some people keep pet mice. They get these mice from pet stores to be sure they are free of diseases, though.

House mice reproduce so quickly that they can overrun a house or even a neighborhood. House mice can carry diseases. House mice can also pollute food with their solid waste. Even though wild house mice can cause a lot of problems, many people like to keep pet house mice that they buy at pet stores!

Mice are used in lab studies because they are easy to care for and reproduce quickly.

House mice are quick, small, and good at hiding. You might have one in your house right now! If you think that you have a house mouse in your house, there are several clues that can tell you. Look for ripped and torn food boxes. Chances are you will also find their solid waste. You might hear their high-pitched squeaks, their claws scratching, or their teeth gnawing.

> Mice may gnaw on electrical wires. This is dangerous because gnawed wires can start electrical fires.

House mice may look cute, but they can carry diseases that can be harmful to your health. If you think your house has mice, tell your mother or father. Do not try to catch mice by yourself.

GLOSSARY

AGILITY (uh-JIH-luh-tee) The property of being able to move around quickly and easily.

DEFEND (dih-FEND) To guard from being hurt.

GNAW (NAW) To keep on biting something.

MAMMALS (MA-mulz) Warm-blooded animals that have a backbone and hair, breathe air, and feed milk to their young.

MATE (MAYT) To come together to make babies.

OMNIVORES (OM-nih-vorz) Animals that eat both plants and animals.

POISONS (POY-zunz) Matter that can cause pain or death.

PREDATORS (PREH-duh-terz) Animals that kill other animals for food.

REPRODUCE (ree-pruh-DOOS) To have babies.

SPECIES (SPEE-sheez) One kind of living thing. All people are one species.

SUBURBAN (suh-BER-bun) Having to do with an area of homes and businesses that is near a large city.

SURVIVE (sur-VYV) To continue to exist.

TUNDRAS (TUN-druz) Icy lands of the coldest parts of the world.

URBAN (UR-bun) Having to do with a city.

INDEX

WEB SITES

For Web resources related to the subject of this book,
go to: www.windmillbooks.com/weblinks
and select this book's title.